WEATHER CLUES IN THE SKY

CLOUDS

BELINDA JENSEN

illustrations by Renée Kurilla

series consultant: Lisa Bullard

Millbrook Press/Minneapolis

To all of my fabulous friends who help me keep my feet on the ground and my dreams in the clouds. To my dear Monique who always made me smile and soak in every minute of sunshine and life. —B.J.

For everyone who loves to picture animals in the clouds as much as I do. —R.K.

Millbrook Press
A division of Lerner Publishing Group, Inc.
241 First Avenue North
Minneapolis, MN 55401 USA

For reading levels and more information, look up this title at www.lernerbooks.com.

Cloud background: © Vodoleyka/Shutterstock.com.

Main body text set in ChurchwardSamoa Regular 15/18.
Typeface provided by Chank.

Library of Congress Cataloging-in-Publication Data

Jensen, Belinda. author.
    Weather Clues in the Sky: Clouds / by Belinda Jensen ; Renée Kurilla, illustrator.
        pages cm — (Bel the Weather Girl)
    Includes bibliographical references and index.
    Summary: "Bel and her cousin, Dylan, explore clouds, learning about different cloud types and how they form" —Provided by publisher.
    Audience: 005-007.
    Audience: K to Grade 3.
    ISBN 978-1-4677-7963-0 (lb : alk. paper) — ISBN 978-1-4677-9745-0 (pb : alk. paper) — ISBN 978-1-4677-9746-7 (eb pdf)
    1. Clouds—Juvenile literature. I. Kurilla, Renée. illustrator. II. Title.
QC921.35.J46 2016
551.57'6—dc23

2015015835

Manufactured in the United States of America
2-42166-18681-5/4/2016

TABLE OF CONTENTS

Chapter One

The Soccer Tournament

Bel wiped her forehead. "It's so hot. I hope we make it through our final game."

Her cousin Dylan looked up. "The sun is better than those clouds. They could mean a storm. Then no more soccer!"

"That would stink," Cody said. "Just like last tournament! First clouds, then thunder. Then we all got sent home."

"Those aren't storm clouds, guys," Bel said. "Here, I'll show you. Weather isn't so mysterious once you understand it!"

She led the boys over to where Lily was drawing with sidewalk chalk. "What's up?" Lily asked.

"We're afraid we'll be rained out," Cody said. "But Bel the Weather Girl is going to explain why not."

Sometimes clouds are made by airplanes. These long, thin clouds are called contrails.

Chapter Two
Cloud Creation

"When the air near Earth heats up, it rises," Bel said. "It carries moisture from lakes, rivers, and oceans."

Dylan laughed. "Maybe moisture from our sweaty jerseys too!"

THE WATER CYCLE

WATER AND ICE CRYSTALS

RAIN

RISING MOISTURE

"The air cools as it rises," Bel said. "Drops of water form around pieces of dust. If the air rises high enough, ice crystals form. Those drops of water or ice crystals turn into clouds."

"Clouds all start the same way. But they don't end up looking the same," Bel said.

Dylan pointed at the sky. "Yeah, there's a dolphin. And that one's an eagle."

Bel laughed. "I mean that different kinds of clouds look different. Some form high up, and some hang down low. Some are puffy, and some are flat. Those are all weather clues!"

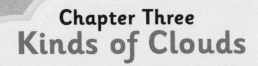

Chapter Three
Kinds of Clouds

Bel picked up some chalk. "See how today's clouds are thin and wispy? And up really high? They're called cirrus clouds."

Cumulus clouds are flatter on the bottom and puffy on top.

Lily drew puffy white clouds on the sidewalk. "So what about when the clouds look like big cotton balls?" she asked.

"Or turtles?" Cody added a head and feet to one of Lily's clouds.

"Those are cumulus clouds," Bel said. "If they're not very tall, it usually means nice weather."

"But sometimes, cumulus clouds grow super tall. They turn into dark cumulonimbus clouds," Bel added.

Dylan colored Lily's clouds so they were gray and towering. "Are they monster clouds like these? They mean thunderstorms, right? I hate storms!"

Cumulonimbus clouds are dark gray because they hold so much water.

Bel nodded. Cody raised his hands like claws. "Grrrrr! Watch out for the cumulonimbus!"

"Sometimes the sky looks like a gray blanket," Cody said. "What clouds are those?"

"Low, flat clouds are called stratus clouds," Bel said. "Stratus clouds form when wet air rises slowly. They can bring light rain or snow."

When a cloud is so low it touches the ground, it's called fog.

Chapter Four
Game Time!

"Hey, Crickets team," called Coach. "Time to huddle up!"

"Game time and no storm. You were right, Bel," said Dylan. "Weather isn't such a mystery when you read the cloud clues!"

"You've got it," Bel said. "So stay tuned for tomorrow.
Because every day is another weather day.
But for now: go, Crickets!"

Try It: Make a Cloud

What you need:

a large, clean jar

a grown-up to light and hold a match

matches

a gallon-sized zip-top bag filled with ice

What you do:

1. Fill the jar one-third full with warm water.

2. As the water warms the air in the jar, the sides fog up.

3. **Important: A grown-up must do this step!** Have a grown-up light a match and hold it for a few seconds at the opening of the jar. Then the match can be dropped into the jar.

4. Put the bag of ice on top of the jar right away. The warm air rises, cools near the ice, and falls. This creates a water cycle. You will quickly see a cloud begin to form.

5. After about a minute, lift off the ice. Your cloud will rise out of the jar. You are a cloud maker!

Glossary

cirrus: thin, high clouds made of ice crystals

contrails: long, thin clouds that form behind airplanes

crystals: a solid material made of a regularly repeating pattern

cumulonimbus: a high, towering cloud that often produces rain and storms

cumulus: puffy clouds that form when moist air rises quickly

fog: a cloud that is so low it touches or nearly touches the ground

moisture: wetness

mysterious: puzzling

stratus: low, flat clouds that seem to cover the sky

thunderstorm: a storm with lightning and thunder

Further Reading

Books

Hall, Katharine. *Clouds: A Compare and Contrast Book.* Mount Pleasant, SC: Arbordale, 2014.
Compare and contrast different kinds of clouds through the photos in this book.

Lawrence, Ellen. *What Are Clouds?* New York: Bearport, 2012.
Learn much more about clouds in this fact-filled book.

Paul, Miranda. *Water Is Water: A Book about the Water Cycle.* New York: Roaring Brook Press, 2015.
Read about clouds and the water cycle in this picture book.

Websites

PBS LearningMedia: Clouds and Weather
http://www.pbslearningmedia.org/resource/evscps.sci.life.clouds/clouds-and-weather/
This website has a video you can watch to learn more about clouds.

S'COOL: On-Line Cloud Chart
http://science-edu.larc.nasa.gov/SCOOL/cldchart.html
Click on cloud photos to see examples of each cloud type.

Web Weather for Kids: Clouds
https://scied.ucar.edu/webweather/clouds
Visit this website to learn more about clouds and play a cloud matching game.

Index